I once had an uncle called Bob

Who was really a bit of a slob

He did not wash his tool

And a long string of drool

Would perpetually hang from his gob.

There once was a stripper from Strood
Whose act was disgracefully rude
For she liked to unloose
A great tide of abuse
On the tossers by whom she was viewed.

A lady on board the Titanic
Saw it sinking and started to panic
First she prayed to the Lord
Then of men still aboard
Had a hundred and three in her panic.

A Parisian banker named Reine
Went too long of the dollar and yen
And it has to be said
There weren't many tears shed
When he threw himself into the Seine.

A lodger who lived in Porthcawl
Once discovered spot on his ball
He exclaimed: "Goodness gracious!
That cyst looks sebaceous
Or else there's a slut down the hall."

There once was a young lady actor
Who'd contrived to stay virgo intacta
Though she'd got several parts
Shared a flat with two tarts
And had three rich old codgers who backed her.

A guy from LA called Jim Fox
Weighed two seventy pounds in his socks.
As he headed their way
You would hear people say:
"Is that Jim, or some fresh seismic shocks?"

There was an Oxonian named Dodds
Whose chief pleasure was strolling round quads
He was strolling round Tom
When he trod on a bomb -
Well, I ask you, now what were the odds?

Every day, as the sun 'gan to wester,
A Medieval lady from Leicester
Would retire for the night
And be bonked out of sight
By her sumpter, her reeve and her jester,

A lady who lived in Twin Cities
Was incredibly proud of her titties
Every day when she woke
She would give them a poke
And say: "How are you doing, my pretties?"

A Hispanic whore from Topeka
Got to Congress, the clever young chica,
But in less than a day
They had turned her away
For performing an act on the Speaker.

There once was a bishop of Nantes

Who went for a wee in the font -

He was deeply contrite

But God said: "It's all right

You can poo in it too if you want."

There was an old man from Dumfries
Who was fond, not of goose, but of geese -
Every day during autumn
He'd woo 'em and court 'em
Till someone informed the police.

There once was a girl from Mauritius
Whose morals were sordid and vicious.
Female critics weren't kind
But the men didn't mind
Since her figure was simply delicious

There was a young girl from Demoins
Who dressed in a skirt made of coins
Till a moment of lust
When she rolled in the dust
And it all came apart at the joins.

To a Scotsman I once knew named Warren
The whole notion of undies was foreign -
This he tended to find
Quite a bit of a bind
As his bits were too big for his sporran.

There was a man from Mull
Whose mind was slow and dull -
It was all you could do
To get twice two
Is four into his skull.

There was also a man from Staines
Who was born with shit for brains
He spent five years at Eton
Was constantly beaten
And learned sweet FA for his pains.

A lady from Leamington Spa

Had the biggest known bosoms by far

They were so massive that

Two grown men and a cat

Could have sailed round the world in her bra.

The chef of a hotel in Thame,
While chopping shallots, missed his aim;
Though the guests still got fed
His performance in bed
From that moment was never the same.

There was a young man from Arbroath
Was suffered with conjugal sloth
Which is caused, in the main,
By a wife fat or plain
Only *his* wife, poor bugger, was both.

There was a young fellow named Jude
Who sat on a bean in the nude
And it soon came to pass
That from out of his arse
Several shoots had begun to protrude.

There was a young girl named Hedwigge
Who had an incredible figure
Her behind was as round
As a new-minted pound
And her boobs were like footballs, but bigger.

A top biological boffin
Retrieved a fresh corpse from its coffin
He brought it to life
And made it his wife
And now there's a kid in the offin'.

There was a young man from Dunblane
Who could only get pleasure from pain
The most tender caress
Turned him on ten times less
Than a welt from a whip or a cane.

There was a young fellow named Sykes
Who had curious sexual likes
Just a glimpse of a chain
Would drive him insane
To say nothing of collars and spikes.

A Merseyside lass named Corinna
Pulled a bloke from Belgrade at a dinner
And it thus could be said
That, though from Birkenhead,
She'd a great deal of Serbian in her.

A fastidious man named Killkuddy
Rather fancied the bird of his buddy
One fine day in a field
She was ready to yield
But he hated to get his clothes muddy.

There was a young lady named Greta
Who would charge to let anyone pet her
You could have a good feel
For the price of a meal
And for two you could thoroughly vet her.

A horny young couple named Bains
Were mad about shagging in trains
Once they got on at Crewe
And were still in the loo
When they stopped two hours later at Staines.

The second Marchese di Dondola
Once tried to have sex in a gondola
But the girl he had chosen
Was frigid and frozen
And barely allowed him to fondle her.

An inveterate lecher from Bicester
Was insanely in love with his sister
This compounded his sins
And played Hell with his shins
As she kicked him whenever he kissed her.

There was a young man from Berlin
Who believed that to breathe was a sin
And by hook or by brook
For each breath that he took
He would hold the next seventy in.

There was a young lady from Venice
Who was good at two things: sex and tennis
And, as one would have thought,
When she got on the court
She was really a bit of a menace.

There was a young lady from Tring
Who bedizened her fanny with bling
And whenever her pleasure
Achieved proper measure
They heard the result in Beijing.

When she got the itch, Lady Godiva
Paid a serf or a servant swive her
And their usual quote
Was no more than a groat
(Which in modern-day money's a fiver).

There was a young man from Tashkent
Who would break wind wherever he went
And the unkeenest hound
Could have run him to ground
So abominable was his scent.

There was a young man from Hong Kong
Who insisted on wearing a thong
Though the way it would pass
Up the crack of his arse
Made him wriggle and squirm all day long.

A costive young lady from Crewe
Had a naiad who lived in her loo
And each time she'd deposit
A voice from the closet
Cried: "Is that the best you can do?"

There was a young fellow named Lambton
Who used to play prop for Northampton
But he couldn't quite stick it
And moved on to cricket
Where willies get hit, but not stamped on.

There once was a fellow named Foley

Who ate unbelievably slowly

It once took him a day

Just to nibble his way

Through some tacos with cheese guacamole.

There was a young man from Dunkirk
Who was simply an out and out berk
I would try to evoke
All the faults of this bloke
But no words that I know of would work.

There was also a man from Bombay
Who's appallingness blew one away
If I tried to appraise
All his terrible traits
It would take me a year and a day.

There was a young lady from Derry
Who was quite inconceivably merry
But this wasn't a freak
For she drank, every week,
Up to seventeen bottles of sherry.

A musical lady named Shoonah

Had a fling with her harpsichord tuner

His erotic technique

Knocked her into next week

And she came like a train, only sooner.

There was an old man from Strathclyde
Who purchased a Latvian bride.
Being willing and eager
Like most girls from Riga
They did it all night and he died.

There was a young man from Dunblane
Who could only get pleasure from pain
The most tender caress
Turned him on ten times less
Than a welt from a whip or a cane.

I once paid a call on a whore
Who had "Strict Mistress" pinned to her door
By the time we were done
I'd had oodles of fun
But core blimey my bottom was sore.

There once was a limerick from Fife
Whose poetic shortcomings were rife
The third and fourth line
Did not really rhyme
And the fifth one had so many syllables you could have found yourself reading it for the rest of your life.

Printed in Great Britain
by Amazon.co.uk, Ltd.,
Marston Gate.